CONTENTS

ABOUT THE AUTHORS

JOHNNY LEE LANE is Director of Education for the Remo Drum Company where he runs the office from Indianapolis, Indiana. Lane, one of the nation's foremost college percussion educators, was Professor of Music and Director of Percussion Studies at Eastern Illinois University for 28 years. He spent the last three years at Indiana University School of Music at IUPUI. At Eastern, he developed one of the finest total percussion programs in the nation. His students are college teachers, performers, and educators throughout the world. In the 1980s, Lane toured Germany four times and was a very well-known percussionist throughout that country. For 13 years, he was the host and founder of the United States Percussion Camp. This camp was a "total percussion" camp, with over 300 students and 37 faculty members, and was held each summer at Eastern Illinois University. Lane and the camp appeared on ABC's *Good Morning America* show in 1996. At Eastern, Lane taught undergraduate and graduate percussion majors, conducted the percussion ensemble, marimba orchestras, marimba rag bands, and the World Percussion program. He continues to be the Percussion Consultant and teacher of the Tennessee State University Drumline in Nashville, Tennessee.

Lane continues to do clinics around the country for Zildjian, Mike Balter Mallets, Remo Drum Company, Silver Fox Marching Sticks, Grover Pro Percussion, and Dynasty Marching Percussion.

Professor Lane also led the 2004 Tournament of Roses Parade, playing the world's tallest drum.

SAMUEL A. FLOYD, JR. is Founder and Director Emeritus of the Center for Black Music Research, at Columbia College in Chicago. Before launching a career in black music scholarship, he taught percussion at Florida A&M University (1962-64) and Southern Illinois University-Carbondale (1965-1968). He published three books on drumming: *99 Street Beats, Cadences, and Exercises for Percussion* (1961), *101 Street Beats, and Exercises for Percussion* (1965), and *Contemporary Exercises and Cadences for Marching Percussion* (1975), and while teaching privately, began to write the first draft of *Four Mallet Independence for Marimba*. His later career focused on scholarly writing, which produced articles that appeared in several scholarly journals, including, *American Music*, *19th Century Music*, *Music Journal*, *The Black Perspective in Music*, and *Black Music Research Journal*. Among his published books include *The Power of Black Music* (Oxford University Press, 1995), and the *International Dictionary of Black Composers* (Fitzroy Dearborn Publishers, 1999). He is now working toward the completion of a manuscript of *A World History of Black Music*.

THE EDITOR RICHARD L. WALKER, JR. is Director of Percussion Studies at the IU School of Music at IUPUI. He is also Director of the IUPUI Percussion Ensemble, Urban Percussion Ensembles, Afro-Cuban Ensemble, Steel Pan Ensemble and teaches the History of Black Music. Before joining the IUPUI School of Music faculty in 2005, he was coordinator of music business and percussion studies at Winston-Salem State University. Mr. Walker received his Bachelor of Music in percussion performance from Northern Kentucky University and a Master of Music in percussion performance from the University of Illinois at Urbana-Champaign. Mr. Walker has performed with the Phantom Regiment Drum and Bugle Corps, the Arkansas Symphony, the Sinfonia Da Camera chamber orchestra, the Champaign-Urbana Symphony, the Conway (AR) Civic Orchestra, and the Pine Bluff (AR) Symphony. He is in demand as a percussion soloist and percussion clinician. As a performer, Mr. Walker traveled Japan with a percussion ensemble that featured world-acclaimed marimbist Kieko Abe.

Richard Walker has served as Assistant Band Director for the University of Texas-Austin Longhorn Band, Assistant Director of Bands and Director of Percussion Studies at the University of Central Arkansas and Assistant Director of Bands and Director of Percussion Studies at University of Arkansas at Pine Bluff.

Mr. Walker was Educational Marketing Manager for the Avedis Zildjian Company for North America. He currently continues his association with music business as an educational artist-endorser and clinician for the Avedis Zildjian Company and for Mike Balter Mallet Company.

Mr. Walker has an extensive background in music technology and computer software development. He is the author of an interactive CDROM designed to teach percussion rudiments to student drummers.

INTRODUCTION

This book is designed to help students develop four-mallet independence through the concentrated study of progressively arranged exercises. It is written in such a way as to give the student a solid foundation in the independent manipulation of two mallets in each hand. All exercises should be played as written, starting each one slowly and gradually increasing the speed (on successive repeats) to appropriate tempos.

The mallets may be held in the following manners:

MUSSER-STYLE GRIP   OR   TRADITIONAL CROSS GRIP

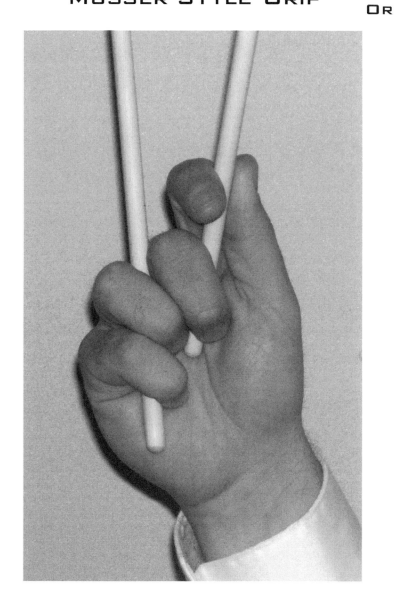 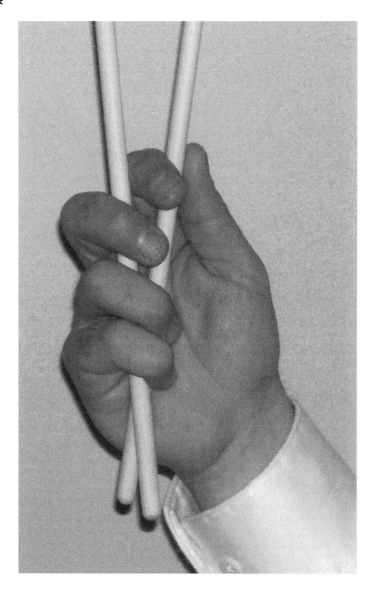

THE MUSSER-STYLE GRIP

The Musser-Style Grip is the most versatile grip. It allows for greater independence, ease, and agility while adjusting the mallets for multiple intervals.

The mallets should be held in the following manner:

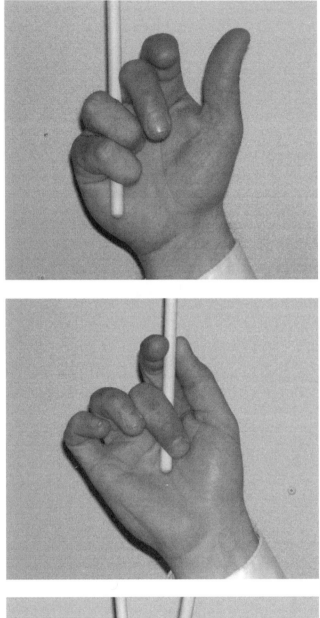

OUTER MALLET

Place a mallet between the middle and ring fingers. Hold the mallet with the ring and little fingers.

INNER MALLET

Put the bottom of the mallet in the palm of the hand. Place and hold the mallet between the thumb and index fingers. Support the mallet with the middle finger.

BOTH MALLETS

The outer mallet is stationary and the inside mallet is movable. Intervals are achieved by supporting the inner mallet with the middle finger while rolling the index finger and thumb to create the desired interval.

With this grip, the mallets may be manipulated as shown below.

For small intervals:

One Hand

Both Hands

For large intervals:

One Hand

Both Hands

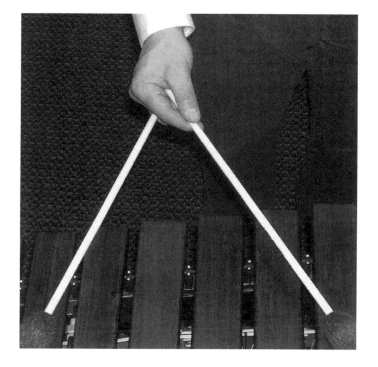

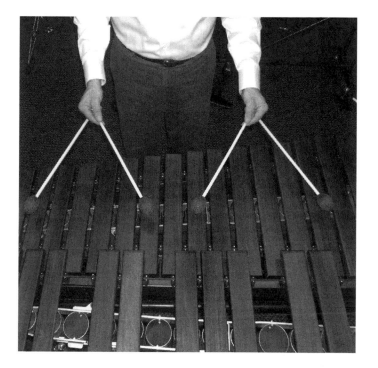

THE TRADITIONAL CROSS GRIP

The Cross Grip, also know as the Traditional Grip, can also be used. It allows for greater four-mallet stability at loud dynamic levels while adjusting the mallets for multiple intervals. This grip also allows for increased stability while playing double stops or chords.

The mallets should be held in the following manner:

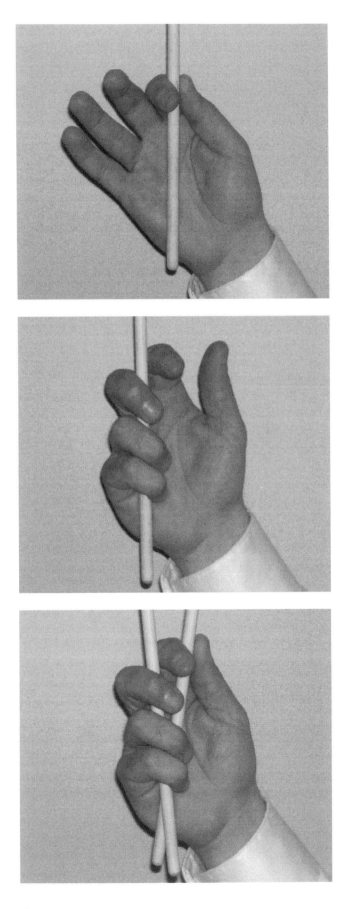

INSIDE MALLET

Place a mallet across of the palm of the hand. Support the mallet between the thumb and index fingers.

OUTSIDE MALLET

Place a mallet between your index and middle fingers. Support the mallet with the ring, middle, and little fingers.

BOTH MALLETS

The outer mallet is placed on top of the inner mallet. The outer mallet is the stationary mallet, and the inside mallet is the movable mallet. Intervals are achieved by placing the index finger between the inner and outer mallets, using both the thumb and index finger to open and close the mallets to create the desired interval.

With this grip, the mallets may be manipulated as shown below.

For small intervals:

One Hand

Both Hands

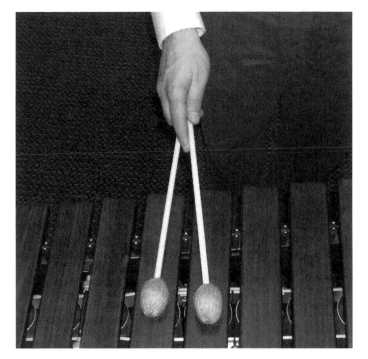

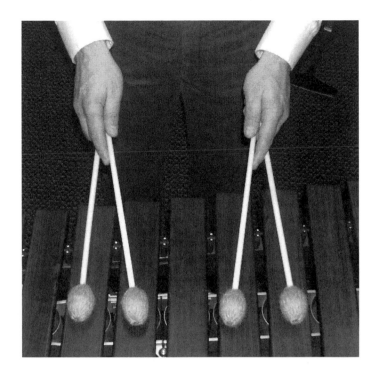

For large intervals:

One Hand

Both Hands

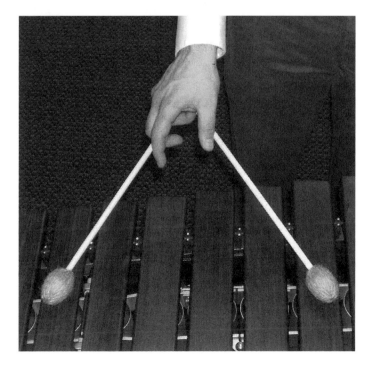

SYMBOLS AND MARKINGS

In this book, certain markings (hand and mallet indications) are necessary. They are illustrated as:

L = Left Hand

1 = Left Outside Mallet

2 = Left Inside Mallet

R = Right Hand

3 = Right Inside Mallet

4 = Right Outside Mallet

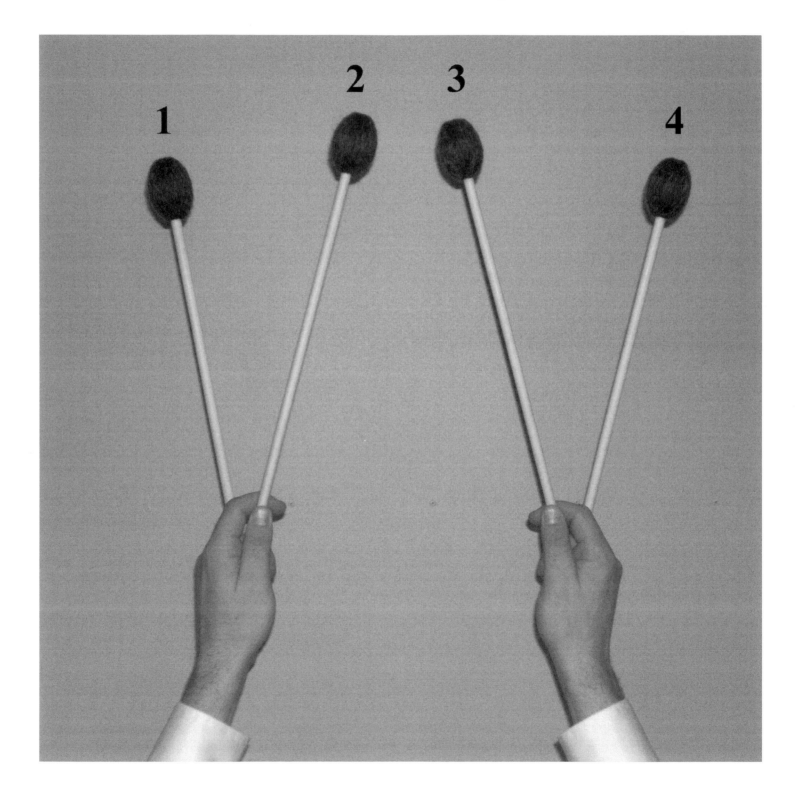

INDEPENDENT MOVEMENT

Examples of four-mallet independent motion are as follows:

Note the wrist rotation for each hand.

MALLETS 1 AND 3 STRIKING BARS SIMULTANEOUSLY.

MALLETS 2 AND 4 STRIKING BARS SIMULTANEOUSLY.

THE ROLL

When using the Musser-Style Grip, a four-mallet roll is produced by striking the bars one hand at a time with two mallets in each hand. As illustrated below, alternating mallets 3 and 4 (right hand) then mallets 1 and 2 (left hand) at a rapid pace produces a "rolling" sound. The "alternating" roll, one single stroke per hand, may be used with both the Musser-Style Grip and the Traditional Grip.

MUSSER GRIP - THE RIGHT HAND STRIKING THE MARIMBA

MUSSER GRIP - THE LEFT HAND STRIKING THE MARIMBA

When using the Traditional Cross Grip, roll as you would when using only one mallet in each hand—alternate the hands. The two mallets held in one hand should strike the bars at the same time.

CROSS GRIP - THE RIGHT HAND STRIKING THE MARIMBA

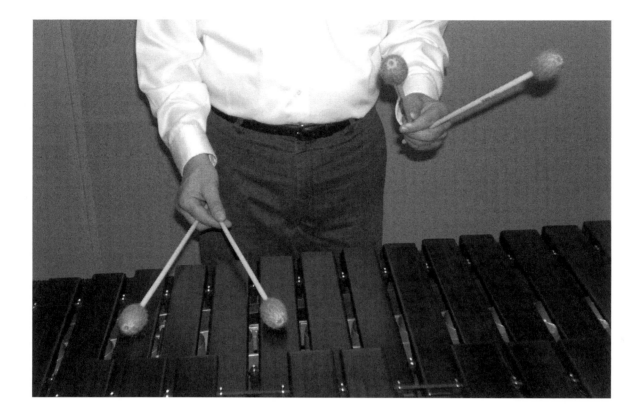

CROSS GRIP - THE LEFT HAND STRIKING THE MARIMBA

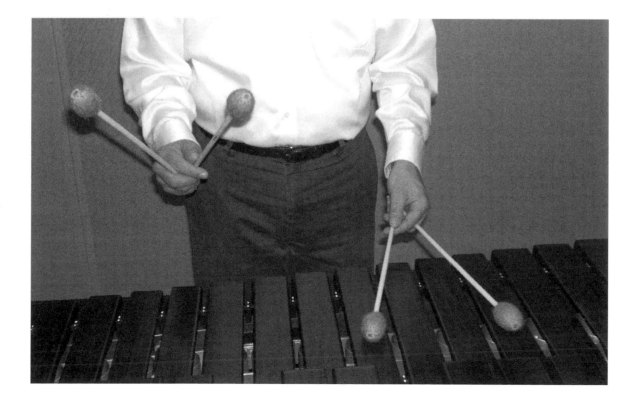

MALLET INDEPENDENCE DEVELOPMENT SECTION

This section will enable individual or independent mallet movement, growth, and development. The exercises begin with working one hand at a time, gradually incorporating the use of both hands. Melodic and chordal structure are introduced (exercises 19–24), followed by one-hand interval drills (exercises 25–32). After playing melodic independent four-mallet studies, the section is concluded by five intermediate-level arranged melodies.

Exercise 1

Exercise 2

Exercise 3

Exercise 4

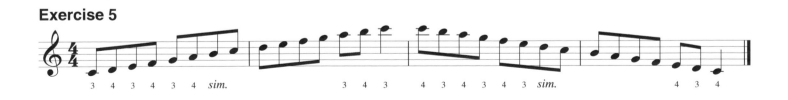

Exercise 5

Exercise 6

Exercise 7

3 4 3 4 *sim.*

3 4 3 4 3   4 3 4 3 *sim.*

4 3 4 3 4

Exercise 8

1 2 1 2 1 2 1 2 *sim.*

1 2 1 2 1   2 1 2 1 2 1 2 1

sim.

2 1 2 1 2

Exercise 9

Exercise 10

Exercise 11

While playing exercise 12, concentrate on all notes sounding even and smooth with a smooth wrist rotation in both hands. Play the entire exercise slowly, then gradually increase the tempo.

Exercise 12

Exercice 13

Exercice 14

Exercice 15

Exercice 16

Exercice 17

Exercice 18

Exercise 19

4 3 4 3 4 3 4 3 *sim.*

Exercise 20

4 3 4 3 4 3 4 3 *sim.*

Exercise 21

Exercise 22

Exercise 23

Exercise 24

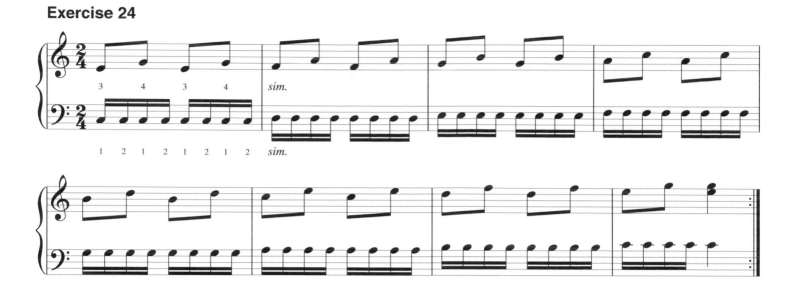

Exercise 25 should be played all the way through, with one hand at a time.

Exercise 25

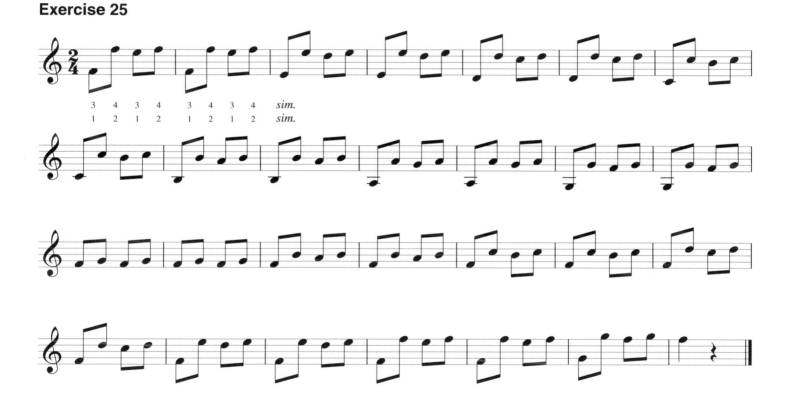

Play exercise 26 with your right hand, then with your left hand.

Exercise 26

Exercise 27

4 1 3 2   4 1 3 2   4 1 3 2   4 1 3 2   *sim.*

Exercise 28

3 4 3 4   *sim.*   4 3 4 3   *sim.*

Exercise 29

1 2 1 2   *sim.*   2 1 2 1   *sim.*

Exercise 30

3 4 3 4 3 4 *sim.*

Exercise 31

1 2 1 2 1 2 *sim.*

Exercise 32

Exercise 33

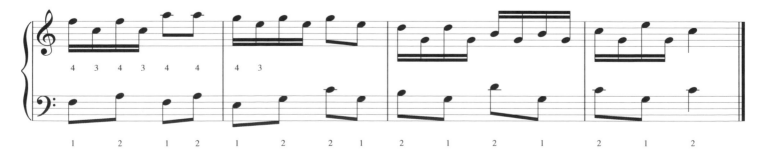

Exercise 34

Exercise 35

Exercise 36

THE ENTERTAINER
(VERSION 1)

SCOTT JOPLIN
Arr. by JOHNNY LANE

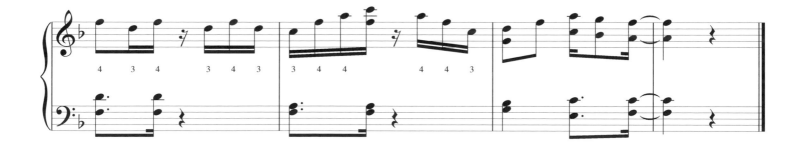

The Entertainer
(Version 2)

SCOTT JOPLIN
Arr. by JOHNNY LANE

25

THREE EXCERPTS FROM CLEMENTI SONATINAS

Op. 36, No. 4

Andante con espessione

Op. 36, No. 3

Un poco adagio

Op. 38, No. 3

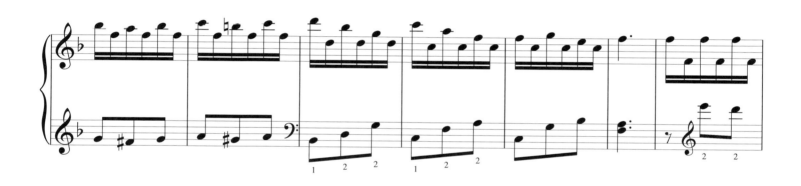

ROLL DEVELOPMENT SECTION

The exercises in this section are designed to help the student develop the ability to move one or the other mallets being held in one hand, from bar to bar, while rolling. The student may find the exercises to be dull. However, hard work and dedication to learning the exercises will result in significantly improved technique. The exercises themselves have been interspersed with simple chorales which will 1) provide relief from the exercises and 2) allow the student to apply the techniques developed as a result of practicing the exercises to musical compositions.

All exercises should be played at least twice. For variety and complete technique development, the "single" notes in exercises 3 through 8 should be played with the inside mallet the first time through, and the outside mallet the second time.

Exercise 1

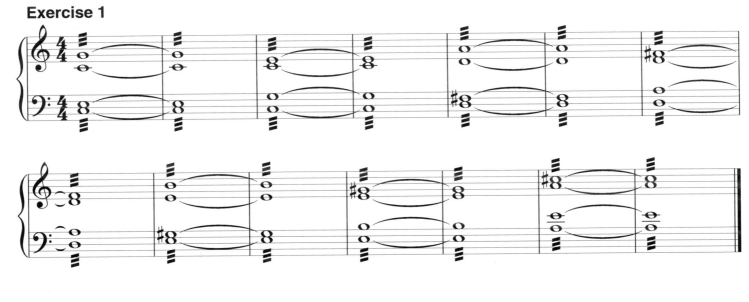

Exercise 2

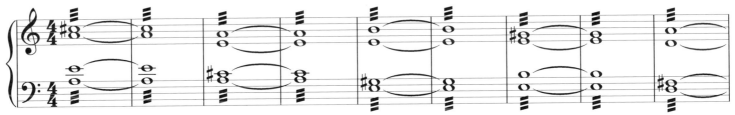
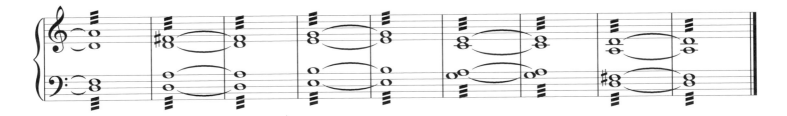

Exercise 3

Exercise 4

Exercise 5

Exercise 6

Exercise 7

Exercise 8

JESU, MEINER SEELEN WONNE
(Jesus, Thou My Soul's Delight)

J.S. BACH
Arr. by TOM SIWE

Roll All Notes

Exercise 9

Exercise 10

Exercise 11

Exercise 12

Exercise 13

JESU, MEINE FREUDE
(JESUS, PRICELESS TREASURE)

J.S. BACH
Arr. by TOM SIWE

Roll All Notes

Exercise 14

Exercise 15

Exercise 16

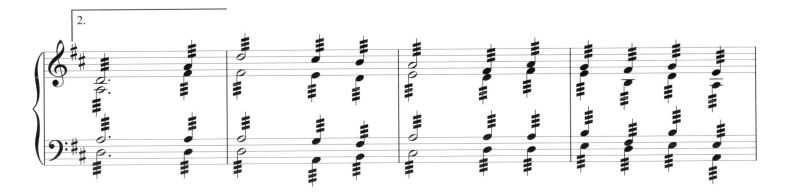

CHRISTUS, DER IST MEIN LEBEN
(Christ, Thou Art My Life)

J.S. BACH
Arr. by TOM SIWE

Roll All Notes

Exercise 17

Exercise 18

Exercise 19

Exercise 20

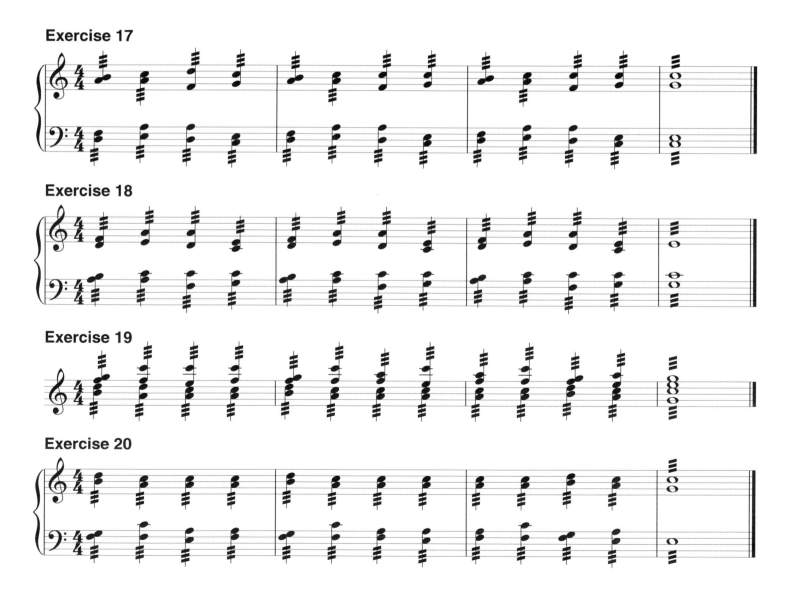

Exercise 21

Exercise 22

O EWIGKEIT, DU DONNERWORT
(ETERNITY, THOU THUNDROUS WORD)

J.S. BACH
Arr. by TOM SIWE

Roll All Notes

Exercise 23

Exercise 24

Exercise 25

Exercise 26

ACH GOTT, WIE MANCHES HERZELEID
(Ah God, How Many a Heartbreak)

J.S. BACH
Arr. by TOM SIWE

Exercise 27

Exercise 28

Exercise 29

Exercise 30

Exercise 31

Exercise 32

Exercise 33

Exercise 34

Exercise 35

Exercise 36

CHACONNE
(from Partita II in D minor for Unaccompanied Violin)

J.S. BACH
Transcribed for Marimba by
JOHNNY LANE

p

tr

f

tr

f

poco rit.

a tempo

p dolce

dim.

pp

f

dim.

mp

dim.

p

mp

cresc.

mf

42

f

cresc.

ff

dim.

poco   a   poco

a tempo   poco rit.

p   *f*   *p*   *f*

p   *f*

broad

cresc.   ***ff***